Midwife Memories
Tales of Amish and "English" Birth Culture

All photos belong to the author with the exception of pictures depicting people. Those photos belong to and were donated by Abby Sugden.

Graceful Beginnings brochure designed by Maggie Wheelock.

Cover design by Renee Popova.

First printing 2020.
ISBN: 9798665486444

Midwife Memories

Tales of Amish and "English" Birth Culture

By Renee Popova

Biography

Renee A. Popova is an internationally known health educator, midwife and consultant. After 30 years of being an advocate for birthing women she retired from catching babies but continues to consult and is available for speaking engagements. Her interest in cultural norms have taken her from Amish religious communities to the maternity hospitals of St. Petersburg, Russia. Renee has appeared on several radio talk shows, television and in numerous newspaper articles.

Names have been changed to protect the privacy of individuals in the telling of their stories and locations have been intentionally vague. Somewhere in Wisconsin…

Contact Info

midwifememories@gmail.com
Facebook Midwife Memories

Acknowledgements

I will be eternally grateful to the women who volunteered to tell their own stories and for permission to include them. I am appreciative of all the midwives who made time for me, encouraged and trained me. A huge heartfelt thank you to **Ciera Levake** for her devotion to editing my work. Her suggestions and comments were valuable in helping me to tell my story. Thanks also go to **Abby Sugden** for the generous offer of photographs and encouragement.

Much gratitude to Deb Anderson for invaluable work at formatting, cover work and all of the polishing she did to help me shine.

Endorsements

The following quotes were by former colleagues of Renee and have previewed the book for review and offered these comments:

"Fascinating insights into Renee's servicing motherhood with great love."
Donna H. Tucson, AZ

"Renee made me laugh, she made me cry; she touched my heart."
Ann H. LaCrosse, WI

"The book is filled with passion and enthusiasm. I was never bored."
Shelly B. Phoenix, AZ

"Renee has been an asset to her community and it's mothers-to-be."
Donald D. Lancaster, WI

"There is a soothing voice and presence throughout the book."
Joy H. Minneapolis, MN

Table of Contents

INTRODUCTION

I have been very privileged to attend the birth of so many babies, both Amish and "English." It difficult to convey the feelings that arise in me when I am at the feet of a woman who is bringing life into this world. It never gets old, or routine, or loses the miracle. Every time I see a little head pop out I am awed by the fact that there is a human being about to emerge into this world. Each mother I am with as she experiences the miracle of birth is etched into my heart and my memory. We bond, we love and we cry together. Many "English" families have continued to send me photos of their children even as they reached adulthood. Amish families do no allow photographs, but none are needed as I also have their stories and experiences imprinted in my heart. To be a midwife is an honor. Women have placed their trust in me and have invited me to share an intimacy that I will treasure forever. I hope as you read this book that you too get a sense of the wonder the miraculous, and the awesomeness of birth.

Chapter 1
I'm Getting Married!

I willingly, and with much anticipation, had my tubes tied when I was just 19. I was married with one child, a daughter, who was not quite two years old. I had been traumatized by the labor and birth experience with my daughter, and I knew I would never take the chance of being that tormented again. A labor that lasted 60 hours, medication that caused me to hallucinate, the use of steel forceps to pull my daughter from me, and 12 hours of separation taught me that childbirth was only something to be feared—and I was going to make sure it never happened to me again.

I met my husband when I was 16 years old. I had been living on my own for several months, and when we met I was certainly taken in by his charm and good looks. We met at a local venue where his band was performing. He seemed so sophisticated and worldly to me, a young naïve girl from a small town in Wisconsin. We immediately had a connection and made plans to spend time together.

Our feelings for each other grew and we continued with our relationship. He was a musician traveling the Midwest and invited me to join him. I didn't need my mother's permission to go as I was already living on my own. Being the young, carefree romantic souls that we were, we decided to marry. As we were traveling, we had to find a community where we could be married in spite of my being underage. We did, and on June 15th, 1973 we became husband and wife.

We didn't want a courthouse wedding, so we drove around and found a church where someone was at home. We spoke with a pastor, and after spending some time with us, he agreed to perform the ceremony. We thought marrying people was one of the duties of a pastor and did not know we were supposed to pay him. It was years later when I realized we should have paid him in appreciation. I feel bad about that to this day.

We thought an outdoor wedding would be nice, so he suggested a location on a bluff overlooking a river. The band members agreed to be our witnesses, and we all arrived at the designated time only to find we would be getting married in a cemetery! The bluff the pastor had led us to had a beautiful view...if we didn't look at all the headstones. We married looking out onto the river, and when we got our photos developed we were shocked to see tombstones in all of our pictures. It hadn't occurred to us that this would be the case, and we laughed every time we saw them. We were off to a great start.

We had been married for about three months when we decided we wanted to have a baby. Looking back, we didn't put a lot of thought into it and what it would mean having a child and living on the road as part of a band. We were in love and taken with the romantic idea of our own baby. My husband made a big production of throwing my birth control pills down the toilet, and we proceeded to enjoy the process of baby-making. Within a few short weeks I was pregnant, and we were elated! Fortunately, by the time our baby came we were no longer traveling and had a stable home for our child.

I had morning sickness that lasted throughout the day, and just the smell of food was hard to handle. Since we were traveling, I would wait in the car while my husband went into a diner to eat as I couldn't bear being around food. The only food I could tolerate was pizza, and so every evening before he went to play with the band he would bring me a few slices. Maybe this is why I still love pizza so much!

I really didn't know what to expect in terms of pregnancy or childbirth. I was the oldest of six children, and you would think I understood something about the whole process, but I was ignorant. Of course I saw my mother pregnant, which to me meant that a baby was coming, but I didn't have a clue. She never gave me the standard "birds and bees" talk, and I don't think I ever asked. It was 60 years before she told me about her pregnancy with me.

When she was pregnant she said she "felt like a million bucks." She grew up on a farm and was used to seeing animals give birth so she didn't feel afraid. Her mother, my grandmother, never talked to her about menstrual periods, sex, or childbirth. Most of mom's information, both fact and fiction, came from the older sisters of her friends. She did some reading about it, but word of mouth was her main source of learning.

During her pregnancy she gained 60 pounds but she lost it soon after having me. She went through 40 hours of labor. She hadn't expected it to be so long but, as we know, there is no way to predict how lengthy a labor will be. She gave birth in a hospital where she was able to walk around her room and stay out of bed for at least a while. At that time it was still standard practice to shave the mom's pubic hair and to be given an enema. Labor became harder of course, and she was not given any type of pain medication. When it was time for delivery, I was pulled out with forceps, and she tells me I ended up with quite a scab on the side of my head. I weighed seven pounds and four ounces and was 19 inches long. I was born around seven in the morning. Mom bottle fed me, and since I was allergic to milk, I was given soy during my infancy. Mom didn't know why forceps were used to deliver me, and I imagine she didn't really ask too many questions.

Chapter 2
My Pregnancy

My husband and I were so looking forward to having our baby. I got books from the library and read as much as I could. I had this vague and uninformed idea of having my baby at home, but there was no support for that notion, and it was quickly dismissed. I couldn't wait until I began to have a baby bump, and I wanted to wear a maternity top long before I needed one. The maternity fashions of the day were hideous with bows at the neck, but I wanted them anyway. I wanted to show off and have everyone around me be as excited as I was. I think most first time moms feel like that.

So anxious were we, that we started attending childbirth education classes when I was only four months along. I'm sure now that we looked silly to the rest of the class participants, but our enthusiasm knew no boundaries. I had read that classes were very important, and classes emphasizing breathing methods were offered through the hospital. I learned a lot, but when I saw a birth video, I have to admit I got a little scared. We took a tour of the birthing ward at the hospital with our class, and I remember hearing some screams and saying that would never be me. Boy would I turn out to be wrong!

Our instructor talked about the birth process, and she used words like "uncomfortable" and "severe cramping." I figured since I had pretty severe menstrual cramps and had dealt with those that I could handle "severe cramping" in labor. Never once did she say "pain." Later on I learned what a liar she was! It was a disservice to me to not tell me there would be pain. When you have pain that is unexpected, you begin to think something is wrong. It starts a whole domino effect of pain, fear, more pain, interventions, pain, and anything but a natural delivery.

One day I was watching my favorite soap opera and there was a maternity room scene. All of a sudden it occurred to me that my baby was going to come out from a tiny hole between my legs. Now this was getting really real!

My pregnancy became more complicated by the fact that my baby was in a posterior (face up) position, and my back was killing me. I spent a week or so in the hospital trying to deal with the pain. have a mild disorder of the spine called Spina Bifida and it contributed to the pain I was experiencing. learned some pelvic tilt exercises, and as the weeks went by I was able to cope. During my pregnancy was an Avon lady selling door-to-door, so I increased my sales calls in order to be more active as my doctor instructed. There I was, going all around the neighborhood toting my bag of perfumes and making sales because my customers got a kick out of seeing me waddle down the sidewalk. When I was hospitalized for the back pain, I took my product with me and made a lot of sales to my nurses. When I see an Avon product now it always takes me back to that time and makes me smile.

Our classes instructed us to prepare for labor by bringing suckers to keep our mouths from getting dry and to bring cards or some other activity to do during labor. With advice like this, you can see how we were set up to experience labor as something that would be "uncomfortable" but manageable to the point of having some play time. How delusional was that teacher and how naive were we!

At quarter to seven on a Tuesday morning, I woke up having some stomach cramps and a few bouts of diarrhea. It took me a little while to realize I was in labor. My back began to hurt, and contractions became regular. We started writing down each contraction as we had been instructed. Contractions were fairly regular at five to seven minutes apart. We went to the hospital to get checked out, and to my great disappointment, we were sent back home to walk and do what we could to make labor stronger.

All day I labored, and while I was getting tired, the pains stayed about the same in timing and duration. That evening we went to a local carnival to walk around and hopefully cause the contractions to increase. Every so often we had to stop so I could hold on to my husband through a contraction. People looked at us as if birth were imminent. I wish it had been. On the way home from the fair we stopped to buy suckers, and I remember being giddy and telling the checkout clerk that we were going to have our baby that night. We were walking on air.

I labored through the night with no changes, and we went back to the hospital on Wednesday for another check. They sent me home again. The pain was getting tough, and we realized it would be more than "uncomfortable." Finally at about four in the morning on Thursday, I was admitted to the maternity unit. Just like back when my mom was having me, I was shaved and given an enema.

Under the instruction of our teacher, we brought a game with us to play, Monopoly. Of course we never took it out of the box. My contractions were now about three minutes apart and very, very painful. I turned into a screamer, and I'm sure I scared my husband. They confined me to bed, except for when I had to urinate. The pain was becoming unbearable. I begged for pain medicine, although I had wanted to have a natural birth. I had figured if it was only going to be "uncomfortable" that I could handle it. Wrong again. I begged for relief, and they finally gave me morphine. I began to hallucinate and saw a large tree growing out of the floor. I was losing my mind. I went into the bathroom to pee and tried to open the window to climb out. I wanted to escape the pain!

After several hours of tortuous labor, they took me to the delivery room. My regular doctor was away since this was a holiday, July 4th. At that time it was not a given that the husband could be present during the birth, but we had done all we could to make that happen. We had gotten our doctor to agree, and it had been a bit of a battle.

I liked my doctor, who I found through the recommendation of my mom's friend who was also pregnant at the time. He was friendly, but looking back I see how totally inappropriate he was. During one of my prenatal visits he was examining my cervix and said, "Boy, your husband sure screwed it in there." I didn't know what to think, and I said nothing.

The on-call doctor agreed to allow my husband in the delivery room, and so he got suited up. I was put on the delivery table, and before my husband came in, the doctor was going to attempt to turn my baby into a proper position. The baby was still posterior, and it would be easier to push and deliver if the baby was face down. I was screaming to be knocked out, but the doctor told me to be quiet and how disappointed my husband would be if I were put out and he couldn't come in the room. I didn't care.

My legs had not yet been strapped down, and when the doctor put his hand in me to turn the baby, I pulled my leg back and kicked him. The last thing I remember him saying was, "Put her out." I never saw that doctor again as he did not visit me postpartum, but sent another doctor instead. Because of my position being flat on my back and the baby' posterior position, along with being asleep, the doctor used forceps to pull my baby out. I was given an episiotomy (a cut to widen my vaginal opening and because of the forceps, my perineum tore all the way to my rectum. Recuperation was so painful because of this tear, and years after giving birth finally had some surgical repair done to correct how badly I had been torn and fixed at the time of birth

I was awakened while I was being stitched. As they wheeled me to recovery, I held my baby for the first time and saw my husband in the hallway. I told him we had a baby girl, eight pounds seven ounces and 21 inches long. She was born at one minute after seven on Thursday, July 4th. She was going to be our own firecracker! He was very emotional and overjoyed. In the recovery room, my baby girl was taken away from me because I had a slight fever from all of the bodily trauma. I did not get to see or touch my girl for another twelve hours. I begged and pleaded, but it fell on deaf ears.

I was in the hospital for a week, and when we finally got home, everything hit me. I was able to breastfeed for a few weeks, and then we switched to a bottle and formula. I became very depressed and I had what we now identify as Postpartum Depression. I had a hard time taking care of my girl and family members stepped in to help. I'm sure none of this reflected well on me in anyone else's eyes, since depression after birth was not talked about, and it was probably easier for everyone to think I just couldn't manage because I was so young. I am forever grateful for family helping to care for her, and their love and care helped me get back on top of things. You know who you are.

I loved my baby girl and loved being a mother, but I knew I could never go through another pregnancy. I was told it would never be like that again, but I could never take the chance. I was petrified of another pregnancy. Severely petrified!

Chapter 3
A Big Decision

My husband and I discussed my great reluctance to have another child. He was very understanding and totally supportive. I experienced two miscarriages before I had my daughter and one miscarriage when she was about a year old. I had not realized I was pregnant when that miscarriage occurred. I was relieved, as I did not want to go through another labor and birth. We agreed that I should get my tubes tied.

We consulted with a prominent gynecologist and he was reluctant to sterilize me due to my age. He questioned us about how we would feel if something happened to our daughter, thinking maybe that would cause us to want another. Since no child replaces another, that argument didn't fly with us. He suggested my husband get a vasectomy, but I was adamant. My husband being fixed did not guarantee I would never get pregnant again. If my husband died or we got divorced, I wanted to be protected. Finally, the doctor said if we waited six months and still felt the same he would do the surgery. Exactly six months later we were back in his office to schedule the procedure.

There are different methods of sterilizing women. I chose to have my fallopian tubes cut and cauterized. Some methods have a failure rate in which pregnancy can still occur. The method I chose had a low failure rate, and I had more peace of mind about it. I was to arrive in the early morning and have the procedure done before noon. I would go to recovery and then be placed in a room for the night and be discharged the next morning.

The room where I was taken after recovery was a large room with four beds for patients. Much to my surprise, three young women were in the other beds, and they were obviously pregnant. I was feeling well after my procedure, and so I struck up conversations with two of the women (the third was very quiet and did not seem interested in talking). One girl told me she was 15 years old. She was six months pregnant and was there for a second trimester abortion. She wore a baseball cap and held a teddy bear. Her parents were with her, and they were comfortable talking to me. They told me she had been pregnant once before and had terminated that pregnancy at five months. She had not told her parents in either situation until she was well along. I couldn't believe what I was hearing. I asked them how many times they were going to do this, and they told me "as many times as necessary." I was shocked and appalled.

During that era it was possible to obtain a second trimester abortion, and sometimes they were not documented as **terminations** for the reason of admission. Sometimes the reason given was 'incomplete miscarriage' and the need to remove fetal tissue.

The second woman who spoke to me was already laboring and couldn't say much. There was a curtain pulled between our beds, and I could hear the sounds of her labor. She was alone. As her pain increased so did her moans, and I could hear her crying. My instinct was to get out of my bed and go to comfort her. I held her hand and tried to soothe her. I don't know how much time I spent with her, but it was a memory I will never forget. She let out a couple of screams, and a nurse came rushing in. She scolded me for being beside the bed and made me go back to my own. After the nurse left I went back to the girl's bedside and tried to console her. It was the first time I felt compelled to help a pregnant woman—and so I did.

Chapter 4
The Calling

I knew that I wanted to be involved with birthing babies since I had my own. Rationally I knew all childbirth did not go like mine. I also knew from personal labor and birth that the experience can shape and affect a woman for the rest of her life. In my case I chose to become sterile. The positive that came out of it was my daughter, but also a desire to help women have the best birth experience possible. I assumed this meant that I needed to become a nurse and work in the obstetrical unit of a hospital.

I applied for nursing school, but at that time there was a two year wait list. I gave up the idea and sought to find satisfaction in another type of work. Years passed, I got divorced from my daughter's father as we had grown apart, and a couple years later I remarried. Time went on, but my desire to help women never left me.

During these years I became a Christian, and my spiritual life flourished. I was feeling the pull to serve pregnant women, and it became a part of my prayers. Many times I discussed this with my husband, and we made the decision that I would go to nursing school as I had once dreamed of. I applied and was accepted for the following semester, four months away.

During my waiting time I studied everything I could about nursing, childbirth options, and the hierarchy within the medical establishment. I learned about the different types of childbirth education and how the philosophy of the method I chose matched my own beliefs. I continued to pray and ask for guidance. The more I learned, the more anxious I became about becoming a nurse. I knew from my own experience, and then from reading and talking to nurses, that the medical field is very regimented and views birth as a medical situation that needs to be managed, as opposed to a natural experience that, in most cases, turns out healthy for mom and baby.

Obstetrical nurses work under the direction of doctors and must follow hospital protocol. This often does not allow the nurse time to be with the laboring mom in a way the nurse might actually like to be. Fortunately, some of that has changed in our current times. I have met so many wonderful and dedicated OB nurses who are very in tune with their patients and their needs and desires. God bless our nurses.

As the time got closer for me to begin the school year, I felt more and more unsure. My husband and I talked and prayed about my heartfelt desire, but also my trepidation. At this point he asked me what it was about working with pregnant women that I really wanted to be doing. My immediate answer was that I wanted to sit at the feet of a laboring woman and serve her. I wanted to be a comfort to her and to celebrate with her. Instantly I knew I could not go to nursing school; my path was in another direction.

Chapter 5
The Path

With great reluctance, I called the school and withdrew from the program. It was the hardest thing I've ever had to do. I wanted it so badly, but I knew I could not serve women as an OB nurse the way was intending to do. I grieved over the loss of being a nurse, but I knew in my heart God was calling me to be a midwife.

Now that the decision had been made not to pursue nursing school, a great burden was lifted—and yet a new burden began. Now I had to figure out what would be my path to becoming a midwife There are nurse-midwives, and there are direct entry midwives (also known as lay midwives). Since I had already ruled out becoming a nurse, I had to start doing research to understand what it took to become a direct-entry midwife. Once again I had to pull out my research books, go to the library, make phone calls to people that I knew who might have some information, and really dig in and find which would be the right path for me. Training as a direct entry midwife was going to be challenging.

Through my readings and conversations with people, I began to understand that a direct-entry midwife held different status depending on the state that she lived in. Many states did not have any rules or regulations governing what type of education or how much clinical experience a direct-entry midwife needed to have. I also found out that a lot of physicians were really suspicious of midwives in their education, and therefore were not very supportive of midwives working in their community. I began to realize that I may be stigmatized in the medical community if I were to pursue the direct-entry route and think about delivering babies at home.

Direct-entry midwives were not allowed to deliver babies in the hospital, and most of the medical community was not at all supportive of home birth. Amish and Mennonite communities, who had their babies at home, were one of the few exceptions. Doctors were willing to provide backup because they understood that, in their case, home birthing was based on religious values. I began to understand that I might become a pioneer in this area as far as my own community was concerned.

I decided that the best way for me to start was to become a childbirth educator and teach childbirth classes. Going through a certification program to become an instructor would be one of the blocks I needed to lay as my foundation for becoming a midwife. I discovered that there were several theories and philosophies of childbirth education. The method that is commonly taught in hospitals mainly focuses on breathing techniques to help a woman cope with labor. I also discovered that these classes taught in a hospital setting often were geared towards preparing the mother and her partner about what to expect when they were in the hospital and, to some degree, to do things the way the hospital wanted them to do it. I knew from my own experience that type of class was not for me.

I felt I had been misled when it came to the realities of labor and birth, and I was convinced the classes I taught would promote a more natural approach. I believed that anyone that was close to the woman could be her coach. I began to discover that I didn't even like the word 'coach' because it reminded me of sporting events and someone on the sidelines yelling and screaming. I knew that was not my approach, and I did not want to educate or support people to behave in that manner.

I looked for and found an educational program that advocated medication-free birth and freedom for the woman to be able to walk and position herself in any fashion that was comfortable for her during labor and birth. That program had an emphasis on the anatomy and physiology of the pregnant body and how it was made to nurture and create a healthy baby.

My study curriculum had an abundance of information on nutrition, which I really appreciated as I had lots of questions about nutrition when I was pregnant, but not a lot of answers. I was only told to limit my weight gain, and of course it did not happen for me as I gained 60 pounds. Having an in-depth course on nutrition was really going to help ne benefit the clients that I would work with.

I discovered it was going to take several months for me to meet all of the requirements to become a certified childbirth instructor, and so I began right away. I contacted the training organization and paid my tuition along with payment for books and any other materials that I would need. There was so much reading to do, and yet with each new book I read, I felt a new sense of empowerment and was motivated to keep going.

One of the requirements was to attend a series of childbirth education classes that were held by a certified instructor. I was able to obtain a list of instructors in my state, and I found a teacher about 30 miles away who welcomed me to come in and attend classes. It was an investment of time and money each week to attend those classes, but that was such a small price to pay for all of the knowledge I was gaining.

Jeannie was a wonderful instructor, and her clients could really relate and feel comfortable with her. She had had a child and was very pleased with her birth experience and wanted to share that with others. My bad experience is what motivated me. I had such high expectations for my birth experience, and all of those expectations were shattered in a very traumatic fashion. I knew that I wanted to help women have a much more peaceful and celebratory experience. I began to realize I really was on the right path towards my calling as a midwife.

Each of the classes focused on a particular aspect of pregnancy and birth. There were classes on anatomy and physiology, the process of birth, nutrition, the birthing experience, breastfeeding and postpartum issues. There was great emphasis on relaxation and preparing your mind and body for the birthing experience. Different types of meditation and stress relaxation techniques were introduced and practiced in each class, and by the end of the 12 week education series, the women found methods they were comfortable with and felt much more equipped going into labor and birth.

So many practitioners speak of it as labor and delivery, but I prefer to think of it as labor and birth. Delivery sounds like you're waiting for a delivery from a retail store or for the delivery of mail. It has such a cold mechanical sound to it, when really it is a glorious birthing of a new life.

I believed non-medicated births were possible and we spent time learning how to mentally prepare our mind and understand that the pain of labor was pain with a purpose. It was not needless pain, pain that produced no results, but it was pain that was bringing forth life. There's such a strong mind-body connection, that being able to work through pain begins in the mind. It's important to have the attitude that the pain I experience gets me one step closer to holding the baby in my arms.

Part of the preparation was learning about meditation and ways to relax the body. During labor, if a woman has the ability to relax her muscles and just let labor happen, she will have less pain. When we have pain our instinct is to tighten up our muscles, grit our teeth, and bear our way through it, but in labor when we tighten our muscles it creates more pain. Oftentimes a partner can be very supportive of the laboring woman through touch and massage, and during the classes we learned how to touch the woman in a way that helped her and would trigger her body's response to relax.

Another important aspect of the childbirth classes was to get the woman and her partner thinking about how she would like her labor to go. Does she want to labor at home until contractions are a certain amount of time apart? Does she want to have other people with her? Does she want to have pain medication? And how will they deal with it if she does not and yet is asking for it? Many women will say they don't want pain medication, and yet understand that they may ask for it during labor. It's important to talk about that ahead of time. Many women will say to their partner, "If I ask for medication, try and distract me and help me through it. If I ask again, then we will talk about it once more." I always helped women understand that just because you have an expectation that things are going to go a certain way, or that you want them to go a certain way, it doesn't mean it will happen. Parents need to remain flexible and realistic.

For the most part I came to understand that drug-free birth is definitely achievable. By the time I finished the 12 weeks of attending Jeannie's childbirth classes, I felt very comfortable moving forward in the role of instructor.

Chapter 6
Training

Another requirement I had left for my certification was to actually attend births and be there as a support person, helping the woman through her labor, as well as the other people that she had chosen to be with her. It was a little tricky trying to find women who would allow me to come and be part of their birth experience. It's not like you can just take an ad out in the newspaper seeking birthing mothers. I looked around in my community and realized that there were some pregnant women in my church. I began to approach them and explain what I was doing and why.

Of all the couples I asked, only one mother denied my request, and I completely respected her decision. There were three other women and their partners who were very open to having me there, and we made arrangements for me to spend time with them prior to going into labor so that I might have a better understanding of their hopes and desires for the birthing experience. I will always be grateful for those women who allowed me to be a part of their most cherished, personal experiences of bringing their children into the world. I learned so much and felt that I was able to contribute, be supportive, and help them achieve the kind of experience they wanted to have.

While I continued to study and work towards the final testing process, I had another requirement for my certification that involved attending a week-long workshop with other aspiring teachers. The workshop that was closest to where I lived was four hours away.

I was lucky enough to have a friend who had a relative living in that area, and my friend decided the week of that workshop was a good time for her to go and visit. Now I had a way to get there and a place to stay. I thoroughly enjoyed my time with my friend and her family, and each day I was anxious to drive to the workshop and see what new bits of information and experience I was going to be a part of.

There were about 40 women in attendance at the workshop, all of them striving to become childbirth educators and perhaps, after that, a doula or midwife. It was wonderful to meet with other women who had common goals, a common philosophy of birth, and were more than eager to share their own birth experiences and what brought them to the point of becoming an educator. I found I was not alone in having had a traumatic birth experience. That was very comforting to me, but it was also sad to understand that so many women had such unpleasant experiences in a hospital setting where the medical establishment's rules tarnished the experience they had in bringing their children nto the world. All of us in that room desired to help women have an experience that they could look back on with peace and joy, knowing that they had been empowered to work with their body, let their body do what it knew how to do, and bring forth life.

At the workshop I had the opportunity to view a variety of birthing videos that showed natural, unmedicated birth. We also saw videos about how cesarean births were handled and how we could best support our clients if they were to have a cesarean section. I returned home excited, motivated, and ready to keep moving full steam ahead. I had met all the requirements to become a certified instructor, and finally I achieved that recognition.

My husband had been very supportive of my desire to become a midwife and was relieved that my confusion and anxiety about nursing school had finally been resolved. In the basement of our house, he created a large classroom in which I could hold my classes. It would accommodate several women and their partners. I purchased office furniture, a copy machine, videos, books, and posters for my classroom. I spent weeks creating workbooks for my clients. So many hours and so much work by both my husband and myself went into creating the perfect environment for pregnant women to come and learn about labor and birth. That effort was worth every minute, every dime, and all of the energy.

Finally, I was ready to begin teaching in my home. We had a local newspaper that was widely read, and I decided to place an ad inviting people to call and inquire about my classes. My town also had a program on cable access television that was always looking for stories from a local angle. I contacted the videographer, and he came to my classroom to interview me. It was a wonderful opportunity to speak about my classes and to show the classroom environment. I was very pleased with the final program that aired.

I didn't know what kind of reception I would get from the community and was pleasantly surprised when I began to get calls. Soon I had several couples signed up for the 12 week classes. I was so excited when it was time for the first class and everyone showed up! The women and their partners came from all walks of life and all were seeking the same thing: education that would empower them to have the natural and safe birth experience they hoped for. Over the next few weeks we really got to know each other and became a tight knit group. I was invited to attend the birth of their babies when the time came and I did so with gratitude and a servant's heart.

While preparing for teaching and midwifery, also studied to be certified as a lactation consultant. An LC is someone who specializes in breastfeeding and is able to guide and assist the new mother in being able to successfully breastfeed her baby.

Many hospitals employ lactation consultants to be immediately available to the new moms and help them to get started with nursing. Babies who latch on to the nipple correctly from the beginning will feed better and mom will not get sore. Breast milk is very nutritious and enables a healthy weight gain for the baby and helps with weight loss for the mother.

Chapter 7
Doulas

The next step in my training to become a midwife was to become certified as a doula. A doula provides emotional, physical, and informationa support to a pregnant woman either in the hospita or at home. She listens to the expectations and desires of the pregnant woman, helping her to make informed choices about what is right for her.

Often a woman will be birthing in a hospital and wants additional support for herself and perhaps a partner or someone else she has chosen to help her. Training and experience enables the doula to build trust and help create an atmosphere allowing the mother to relax and work with her own body. For women who have special needs, a doula can be especially helpful. Those needs might include women expecting twins, vaginal birth after cesarean teen mothers, and first time mothers.

I found a certifying organization that I felt grea about, and once again I had academic and clinica requirements. I also had to attend a variety of doula conferences and was fortunate to meet many women who were following the same path as I was. Afte several months I obtained my certification as a doula and began to attend many hospital and home births By this time I was attending births within 120 mile of my home.

My career has been filled with my role as a midwife, but also as an educator and doula. I really enjoyed when I was asked to be a doula at a hospital birth. Even though a woman may have other people to support her during labor, she is comforted by having someone there to make suggestions, help her to understand options the medical staff are presenting to her, and to offer physical relief such as massaging her feet. A doula can also serve the role of patient advocate, helping the mother to have the type of birth experience she hoped for. Nurses love to be able to offer these things to their patients, but oftentimes the nurse has other patients and her time becomes limited.

A doula is not in the hospital to take the place of medical staff, but to be a part of the team that serves the mother. I have found some hospitals to be resistant to having a doula present. They think the doula will interfere or try to give medical advice. Other hospitals are excited to have a doula come in, as they recognize the more support a laboring woman has, the better. Educating hospital staff about the role of the doula is key to acceptance, and I have spoken to nursing groups and staff about this valuable resource.

Several years ago I helped start the first hospital based doula program in my state. My hospital did not have nurse midwives, and they determined that offering doula services could be a way to provide mothers with a more personalized experience. We developed an intensive training program and reached out to the community for women interested in becoming doula certified. Our hospital foundation assisted in financing the program, and our ultimate goal was to get insurance companies on board and to cover the services. Women who utilized the doula services were very happy with their experience.

Most doulas work independently or within a group of doulas. The majority are not hospital based and need to find clients via word of mouth and advertising. I have traveled to various locations and held workshops aimed at assisting doulas in expanding and marketing their services. Doulas work hard to be recognized as part of the birth team, and acceptance, along with adequate compensation, is oftentimes a struggle.

Chapter 8
More Training

Each state has different requirements for becoming a midwife, and some have none at all. There were no established schools for those without a nursing degree. There were numerous programs offering apprenticeship for varying amounts of time, and these were located across the country. I traveled to Illinois, New York, and Missouri. The path for an unconventional career can be challenging, and sometimes it is necessary to travel for periods of time in order to get a complete academic and clinical education. I also joined a group of lay midwives in my state who met monthly for continuing education and support. We discussed births we had attended, problem-solved, and learned new skills such as neonatal resuscitation.

I was fortunate to meet a couple of midwives who worked with the Amish community, although they themselves were not Amish. Amish communities usually have their own midwives, but if they don't have one, they will work with a midwife outside of the community. Anyone outside is known as "English," and occasionally there will be "English" midwives helping to birth Amish babies. From these midwives I learned new skills and the different cultural aspects of serving the Amish community.

There were many midwives who offered to take me under their wing, allowed me to assist them with

prenatal visits, and tested me on my clinical skills and knowledge. For a long time I felt intimidated by some of the senior midwives. They had been birthing babies for many years, and it was hard for me to grasp that someday I might have the same level of knowledge and skills. Another area of intimidation was the potluck meals that we had at our monthly meetings. Talk about competition! Each midwife tried to outdo each other in the meals they brought to share. Tabouli and tzatziki and hummus, oh my! I had never heard of such foods, let alone prepared them. My contribution was always a loaf of rustic bread from the local
bakery.

As an apprentice, I did everything from reading textbooks, sterilizing instruments, packing birth kits, and practicing my clinical skills over and over and over again. I attended classes held by the midwives and learned to suture, take measurements of the pregnant belly, determine the position of the baby, and how to interpret the baby's heartbeat. Between textbook work and clinical practice, the hours were long and tiring, but very rewarding. I was truly appreciative to have such great mentors, and my education was diverse and thorough due to these skilled practitioners.

Chapter 9
Providing Services

I was meeting pregnant women through the childbirth education classes, as well as being approached in the general community. Referrals were being made to me by other midwives who lived in a different part of the state. We always tried to be supportive of one another and gave assistance where we were able.

I took the business name of Graceful Beginnings, a pregnancy support service. I knew I would be offering a variety of services, and under this umbrella I could offer childbirth education, doula assistance, and midwifery care. It was helpful in advertising and promotion to present myself in a professional manner, and the creation of my services as a business was paramount.

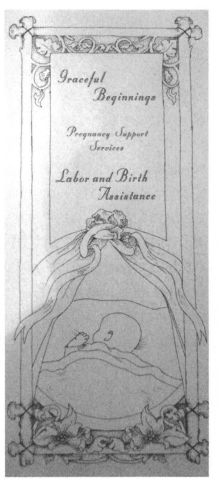

Graceful Beginnings

Pregnancy Support Services

Labor and Birth Assistance

After three years of teaching, working as a doula, and catching babies, I was contacted by a nonprofit community health center and asked if I would be interested in teaching childbirth education to their clients for a six week session. Apparently I had been referred to them by a midwife from that area, and they were excited to have me as part of the team. I created a curriculum for these sessions and for the next two years traveled 160 miles round trip to teach for the health center.

After the first year they approached me about writing a grant proposal for a program to train women from minority communities to become childbirth educators. The center found that pregnant minority women did not attend the general childbirth classes. As this was a very important demographic, the center wanted to reach out to them. I wrote the proposal and we received a grant to cover the cost of writing the curriculum, recruiting the students, and holding an educator training class for eight weeks. I developed the class outline and content, trained four women to become childbirth teachers, and mentored them through their first series of classes. These instructors held classes within their own communities and were successful at getting their friends and neighbors to attend. It was a wonderful and effective way of getting education to the underserved.

Chapter 10
The Amish Come Calling

In Wisconsin there are several Amish and Mennonite communities. I grew up very aware of them, as they were an everyday part of life. I would see the women shopping in town wearing their head coverings and black shoes. The men would frequent farm auctions, and their horses and buggies were tied off to the side of the barn. We would drive by their homes and see children working in the garden and fresh laundry hanging on the clothesline.

At the time I also owned a Christian bookstore, and the women would come in to look around and make a purchase. My husband, daughter, and I were invited to attend Sunday church service and then have lunch with a Mennonite family that I had met through the bookstore. We gladly accepted. We were warmly welcomed and had a wonderful day. We learned more about each other and remained friendly for many years.

I didn't set out to become a midwife to the Amish and Mennonite communities, but it happened over time as word spread that I was available. I had some experience with them from when I was being mentored by other midwives, but those families and midwives were in another part of the state.

When I was invited into an Amish or Mennonite home, I always chose to wear a dress rather than my usual pants. I also didn't wear makeup when I went to see them. These changes I made out of respect for their culture.

One day there was a knock on my door and standing on the porch was a Mennonite man in a blue shirt with suspenders and a dark hat. He asked if I was the midwife that he had been told could help him. His wife was going to have her baby at the hospital, but they wanted to go home immediately after the birth. They hoped I could take them home and stay for a while to look after mom and baby. I was taken aback by this request. I had only been apprenticing and assisting at births and didn't think anyone would look for me. I was also surprised they were having a hospital birth, since this was not the norm in their culture. I agreed to meet his wife, and when the time came, I drove them home from the hospital and stayed for several hours. It was my real introduction into working with the religious community.

If I was going to work with the Amish and Mennonites, I felt it was important to gain some cultural insight into their beliefs and birthing practices. I wanted to be able to meet their needs and be respectful of the culture. The Mennonite families I had interacted with had been very open to conversation and questions. They also recommended some reading material, and I was grateful for their willingness to share with me. I especially wanted to recognize opportunities in which the nursing staff could help couples retain their birthing customs if hospitalization was needed.

A whole new world opened up to me as I learned more about the Amish. They are fundamental Christians who came to America from Europe to escape persecution for their religious beliefs. Amish believe in the Bible and live according to the Word of the Bible. Most of us only know the Amish as the people who drive buggies and wear dark clothes and bonnets. They are known as "Plain People." There are several denominations within the Amish, ranging from the Old Order to Mennonite. Old Order members are conservative and quite private. Interaction with outsiders is very limited. The Mennonites are more liberal and interact with the outside world a little more. The Mennonites may drive cars and have electricity in their homes.

Amish people believe they are called to live apart from the world. Clothing is plain and unadorned. Some denominations forbid the use of buttons, and clothing is fastened with straight pins. They live with few conveniences, but they may hire a driver to transport them if necessary or may even ask to use a telephone. The owning and use of modern conveniences may take their focus off of God and may even be considered a waste of money. Amish are frugal people, humble, and hardworking.

Amish families are large, and even the small children are taught to work and be helpful. They can help set the dinner table or pull weeds in the garden. Work is sun up to sun down, and there are no days off. Animals need to be fed and cared for. Amish communities have their own schools which end at the eighth grade. At that time the children are needed at home to help with family work and chores. Families don't see much need for further education, although sometimes exceptions are made. Occasionally a member may be allowed to pursue schooling in order to learn skills that will benefit all families. The community functions as one. We have all seen photos of the Amish building a barn in a day. They support each other in good times and in bad. They are quick to help in times of illness or hardship. If an Amish farmer breaks his leg, his community will arrange to take over his chores and milk his cows. They extend themselves to the English world to help in times of disaster, such as a tornado or fire. When the Covid-19 pandemic was at its most active, Amish women sewed thousands of face masks to donate to hospitals.

The Amish gather in each other's homes on Sunday for worship. It is also a time for sharing a meal and catching up on news. The Mennonites tend to have a church building where they meet, but it varies from community to community.

Amish women choose to have their babies at home because it is in line with their culture of self sufficiency and privacy. Birth is viewed as a natural

event, and they see no need for doctors and hospitals. If their midwife suggests they see a doctor or need to transfer to a hospital, they are usually willing to do so. Most physicians are willing to work with Amish patients should it become necessary to come to the clinic or hospital. Amish women are quite confident in their ability to give birth. Because large families are the norm, sometimes a woman will have given birth eighteen times. There is little complaining about pain, and they are active during labor. They know it will be hard work, and they just do it. They anticipate all will be well, but if it isn't they are accepting and believe it to be God's will.

Amish women do not smoke, drink, or take drugs. They rely on herbs and vitamins to help keep them healthy. They are not concerned about gaining weight and often will gain a large amount. Prenatal care is not common. When an Amish community has to use an English midwife, she is treated with respect and welcomed into the community. Occasionally, the midwife is called by the Amish for other medical issues, as they trust the midwife and already have a relationship. If one of the men falls and cuts his leg on the barbed wire fence, the midwife may be asked to stitch up his wound.

When I was caring for several pregnant women in the community, I broke my leg and had to send them letters informing them of my accident and that another midwife would call on them to assist with

their births. A few week[s] later I sent them all letter[s] stating when I woul[d] return to the communit[y] and resume home visit[s] When I went back to wor[k] the first home I stopped a[t] had a surprise for me in th[e] kitchen. While I had bee[n] laid up with a broken leg my Amish families hel[d] a shower for me and th[e] countertop was filled wit[h] home canned fruits an[d] vegetables, pastries an[d] pies, and even a butchere[d] chicken. I was presente[d] with a scrapbook that eac[h] family had contribute[d] to. It was made fro[m] cardboard, quilt batting lace, and a fuzzy tedd[y] bear. Inside were poem[s] jokes, pictures cut fro[m] magazines, and hand colored flowers an[d] birds. There were tin[y] little envelopes glued o[n] a page, and inside eac[h]

44

one was a tiny note or poem. Personal messages were written to me not just by the pregnant mothers, but by grandparents and other members of the community. There were messages from people I did not know, and one of them said, "Thank you for helping our young mothers in their time of need and of trials. Keep up the good works." My heart was filled with love and gratitude for these people who had welcomed me and cared for me as one of their own.

When an Amish couple wants to connect with the midwife, they send a letter or make a phone call. Usually the husband makes the contact and this happens about eight weeks before the baby is due. Prenatals for the last few weeks are done in their home. Other children are not present as privacy is a great concern. Fathers are very involved and quite attentive. The fathers do much of the talking and negotiating the fee. Payment may be cash, baked goods, farm animals, quilts, furniture or some other form of trade.

There is much preparation to be done. Clothing, bedding, and other linens must be gathered. Supplies must be purchased and some items sterilized. The midwife informs the family of what they need to buy or do so they will be ready before the birth. Arrangements are made for the other children to be taken to Grandma's house and for someone to come and stay after the baby is born. It is also decided when and how to contact the midwife and let her know it is time to come.

During labor a woman walks and stays active. She may sit with her feet in water believing this will cause labor to progress. When the time comes she squats or moves into a comfortable position, and the baby is born into a quiet, peaceful room lit by a kerosene lamp. The father is usually right beside her, encouraging her and soothing her. The three of them now get to know each other.

Mom will breastfeed for many months, and it is viewed as natural family planning. This is often unreliable, and their children can be born quite close together. They do not believe in birth control such as pills, condoms, etc. While birth control is frowned upon, sterilization may be an option. The couple never discuss it with anyone else other than the midwife. The decision is reached more easily if the woman is anticipating a cesarean section. A doctor is consulted and plans are made.

Birthing in an Amish home presents challenges. There is no electricity, water must be pumped, and perhaps there is only a cell phone brought by the midwife. Complications can mean a transfer to a hospital. Complications may arise from genetics, diet, labor events such as fetal distress, or the unknown. Back-up plans must be made in advance. I always told my clients at the first visit that if for any reason I said they needed to see a doctor or to be transported to the hospital, they would need to trust my judgment and comply. An emergency situation is not the time to hash it out. They hired me for my expertise and needed to heed my advice if a quick decision had to be made. They all agreed. In all the years I worked as a midwife, I only had to transfer a mother one time, as she needed a cesarean section.

If medical personnel understand the Amish belief system, the movement to the hospital setting is smoother. Amish have the same fears and concerns as anyone else in the hospital. They have the same desire for a healthy baby. Privacy is very important, and Amish families are very modest. The women want to be covered and will wear their head covering. I never ask the baby's name until after birth. The mother will dress the baby, and photographs are never allowed. There is no health insurance in case of hospitalization. Payment plans need to be made, although sometimes the community will come together and pay the bill. It's always important to explain what we are doing and why. This is not the time to ask questions about their beliefs or customs.

Chapter 11
A Midwife is Born

The first Mennonite family that I served as a midwife came to me by way of a previous contact. Their first child was born in a hospital, and I had taken them home and stayed with them. They were expecting their second in a few weeks. The baby was to be born into peace and love in their home. I had gotten to know this family, and we were quite comfortable with each other. I was a little nervous because this would be the first birth I would do on my own, not as an apprentice. But I was confident in my ability, and the mother was very healthy and well prepared. At a previous prenatal visit we had spoken about how she might want to labor, and now the father was actively helping her to relax. After a few short hours the baby was born into a quiet and dimly lit room. The sweet little boy came into this world without crying. He was awake and alert. My assessment of him told me he was healthy, and he was able to breastfeed right away. I stayed with the family for several hours to monitor mom and baby. Both were doing well, and it was time for me to leave. I informed the parents that I would come back in 12 hours to do a follow- up visit.

When I returned later that day, I found mom to be feeling sick. She was having intestinal issues and was running a slight fever. At first I thought perhaps she was just exhausted and was a little run down. I stayed, gave her fluids for hydration, and continued to monitor her. The baby was doing well and showed no signs of sickness. The husband was also doing well, although concerned that his wife was sickly. Mom's condition stayed the same with fever, and she was becoming weak.

The couple were farmers and kept a phone out in the barn, so I went out to call the midwives I had apprenticed with to ask their advice. I went through what had taken place in regard to the birth, and we did not feel her illness was birth related. It may have been a coincidence that she got sick after giving birth. They suggested I continue with all the measures I was doing for her and see what would happen in the next couple of hours as long as she did not get worse. She was stable, but not feeling better.

After an hour I called our local hospital and spoke with an obstetrical nurse in the birthing center. I told her who I was and gave her the details of the birth and mom's sickness. She said to bring her to the hospital if her fever went higher. For the next few hours she remained the same and was able to sleep for a while.

By this time it was very early morning, and I went to lay down for a brief moment. I realized that I would need to take her to the hospital. I began questioning everything I had done and looking at all of the notes I had made during labor and in the hours following. I asked myself what I might have done wrong or if I had missed something. I knew my time with her would be scrutinized when we went to the hospital, and I needed to be able to answer all questions and concerns. I wrestled and prayed for answers. I asked God to show me what the problem was. I was in prayerful agony.

I questioned whether or not I should even be a midwife. I had never been able to call myself midwife the entire time I was apprenticing. I had not felt worthy. How could I now use the word midwife when I had a sick client and it could have been my fault? I continued to pray, and soon I felt peacefulness come over me. I heard a voice in my head ask me what "midwife" meant, and I answered "with woman." The voice then said to me that in the last day I had been more "with woman" than I would ever be again. I was assured that I was, in fact, midwife. I knew this voice was God speaking into my heart and my mind, and I was soothed.

We drove to the hospital and were immediately seen by a doctor. He was a doctor that I had seen for my own health on several occasions. I liked him and knew he would take great care of the mother. He questioned me about the pregnancy, labor, and birth. I informed him of the timeline for the sickness setting in and what I had done to care for her. Some blood tests were ordered, and as we waited for results, the mom was hooked to an IV and given fluids to replace what she had lost.

The doctor soon returned and turned to me and said that I should be assured I had done nothing wrong. The lab results showed that the mom had salmonella, a bacteria. The doctor informed me that there was no way I could have known without a lab test, and I had done the right thing to bring her in for antibiotics. Apparently, the mom and her family were used to drinking unpasteurized milk from the cows they raised and usually had no problems doing so. It was a guess from the doctor that the physical stress of giving birth caused the mom to be unable to process the milk and she was sickened by it. After a few hours of IV fluids and antibiotics, I was able to take the family home to rest and recuperate. Very quickly mom returned to health, and the baby thrived.

I was shaken to the core by this situation. I had doubted all I had done, but in the end I actually became much stronger in my belief that midwifery was my spiritual calling. I was now comfortable calling myself a midwife and moved forward in faith. I was willing to sign birth certificates when other midwives were not. They were afraid to expose themselves, since the law was not exactly clear on the status of midwives. They would have the father sign the certificate. I signed because I knew I was called to do this, and I would not be afraid. If it led to legal consequences, so be it. I was learning to trust that

small voice that led me when it came to caring fo
my pregnant clients. Trusting that voice was going
to serve me more than I could have known when
later took an "English" couple to be my clients.

Chapter 12
Intuition

A young couple was referred to me and drove some distance to have our first meeting. The mother appeared very healthy, and they both seemed prepared and enthusiastic for a home birth. She was about seven months pregnant and had seen a doctor for a couple of prenatal appointments. After our second visit I began to feel very strongly that she needed to go back to the doctor and that I could not continue as her midwife. I didn't know why I felt this way. The baby's heart rate was good, and she measured appropriately. The baby was active and moving, but I was perplexed by my feelings of unease. The woman was healthy, and there was no logical reason for my reluctance. She was not happy about my decision, but I was firm. I knew I needed to trust my intuition in order to serve her, and I transferred her records to the obstetrician she had seen previously.

I was informed a month later that she had gone into labor and the baby had died shortly after birth. There was a genetic chromosomal abnormality that was not survivable and was not detectable prenatally. I was so saddened for her and her husband. I could not have known and nothing could have prevented it. This very sad situation confirmed to me that I must listen to my instincts—listen to that small voice—and I would be guided in the way I should go.

Chapter 13
Intimidated

As a midwife I couldn't predict who would be brought into my life. Sometimes a woman wanted to have her baby at a hospital but wanted me to be with her as she labored at home until she was ready to go there. Even though a woman may have had her husband or someone else with her, she still could use another pair of hands and another voice to calm and encourage. Oftentimes I ended up going to the hospital with her.

I was asked to attend home labor by a wonderful couple who already had one young son. They were very educated about the birth process and wanted to remain home until closer to birth. I recall this story not only because I liked this woman very much but also because when I arrived at her home there was another person present—her father, who was an obstetrician! In fact, I knew him as he had been in the same practice as the doctor who attended the birth of my daughter and had cared for me during one of my prenatal appointments.

I must say, I was intimidated and tried not to show it. Here I was in the bedroom assisting his daughter in labor, and he was in the next room! Would he question me? Test me? Challenge me? All these thoughts ran through my mind. Many obstetricians do not trust midwives, and now I was attending to one's daughter. I sucked it up and focused on my client, trying not to think about her father. I became so focused on working with her that soon I forgot about him, and in the end, he never said anything other than 'hello.' It was an issue only in my own mind. Mom went to the hospital and birthed a beautiful healthy baby boy.

Chapter 14
Vickie and Brett

Many of the couples I have worked with hav become my friends and stayed in touch all thes years. One couple gave me the honor of attendin two of their births. For the first one I was to assis their midwife, and as for the second...
Brett and Vickie agreed to write their birth stories fror each of their perspectives and gave me permissio to include them in this book. I will also provide m memories.

Vickie's Remembrance: Israel's Birth

"I first met Renee at a local church when I wa pregnant with my fourth son. I attended a birth clas which Renee taught. Renee ended up in the bac end of a station wagon with me in labor on our wa from my home to the town where my midwife livec My husband was driving, and Renee was lying in th back with me trying to get me to relax and breath and not push, which I really wanted to do! W arrived, and shortly after I gave birth in my midwife home, who happened to be married to my prenate doctor. Quite a situation! My son was my first vagine birth and natural birth after three previous cesarea sections at hospitals."

Brett's Story

"Wow! 25 years ago. A long time, memories play tricks and I don't remember much of what Vickie just described. I remember the birth, of course, and the car ride with Vickie and Renee in the back. It was a very powerful birth experience in our midwife's living room with the midwife, Renee, and the doctor awake in the next room just in case. I recall that Vickie squatted for the birth."

My Recollection

At this time I was still in midwifery training and not ready to attend a birth on my own. Vickie and Brett were in my childbirth classes, and we really had a lot in common. They invited me to be at the birth with their midwife. The midwife lived some distance away so most of Vickie's laboring was at their house. I was there with her, and all of a sudden her labor got much more intense. We got Vickie situated in the back of the station wagon, and I climbed in with her. Brett drove. He was pretty calm and steady. Vickie was progressing quickly, and I was trying to reassure her, reminding her to breathe and asking her not to push. It occurred to me that this child might be born in the car and I may catch my first baby! Much to my relief we made it to the midwife's house, and shortly after, Vickie squatted and pushed her beautiful son into this life. So exciting, and boy

was I glad she hadn't birthed in the car! We all tried
to rest afterwards, and I don't ever remember feeling
so exhausted. I think the stress of the situation made
me tired, and I slept as if I had been medicated. Pure
exhaustion.

Vickie's Remembrance: Elisha's Birth
    "Renee continued to pursue her studies in
midwifery, and by the time my fifth son was near
birth, there simply was not any question that I wanted
her to be a part of it. I was going to use a different
midwife, but Renee was going to be with me at my
home. My midwife was also my prenatal caregiver,
and she lived a couple of hours away. Because of
the distance she did not make it in time for the birth.
    "I was late with my son, as I had been with
all my children! Of course with the c-sections
had previously, doctors wanted to take me at their
convenience rather than wait for me to go into labor.
With this pregnancy I was three weeks overdue! My
midwife gave me some homeopathic tabs to dissolve
under my tongue and told me it would not start my
labor but would help me go quickly when I did start.
I do not remember the name of the tabs. As soon
as Renee heard I was in labor she came right over.
I took a long hot shower because labor was strong
and intense and progressing quickly. My husband
Brett was with me, and Renee was downstairs in a
bedroom setting up for delivery. We lived in an old

cheese factory in the country near where I taught art in the local public schools.

"For some (Godly) strange reason, Renee told me she put oxygen with a baby wand in her birth bag before leaving home. We were all set up to deliver on our bed with appropriate plastic and cloths, etc. Labor was soooooooooo......intense...... that at the last minute I hopped off the bed and squatted him right out into somebody's hands and all over the carpet. LOL. But...he was not breathing! I was sooooooo scared, but Brett and Renee started rubbing his wee body, and Renee used the baby wand of oxygen on him. We were all praying like crazy in Jesus' name! I couldn't tell you how long it took, but he started breathing! I got cleaned up, into bed, and the midwife arrived too late for delivery. I have always felt bonded to Renee. I am 100% certain that these birth experiences are why."

Brett's Story

"I remember Vickie going into labor, and that the midwife was called but didn't make it in time. I remember Renee, Vickie, and myself were downstairs in the bedroom and Vickie squatting on the floor again at the last minute. I don't remember catching him, so I'm pretty sure Renee did. I definitely remember the immediate seriousness and gravity that came over the room right after the birth, but I don't recall Renee saying anything. Of

course she must have said something. I don't thin
I was rubbing him either, that was all Renee. I ver
much do remember immediately going into praye
and just as immediately I was filled with peace. Th
entire room was being filled with a heavy presence c
grace. It was so real, so alive, I could feel it in ever
sense of my being, and I knew everything was goin
to be fine. Our boy started breathing. He was o
in every way measurable, and we soon celebrated
beautiful, wonder-filled birth. It was because of thi
experience of God's grace upon us all that Vicki
and I decided to name Elisha's middle name Grace
The old testament prophet Elisha was a man tha
received double God's grace, and that is exactl
what we believe he did for our Elisha! I remembe
this was Renee's first non-Amish birth alone, and i
was our first home birth in our own home."

My Recollection

I didn't normally carry oxygen to a birth whe
I was just planning to assist because the midwif
would have all of her equipment, but something
told me to bring it. Things were calm when I arrive
at the house, and Vickie was in active labor. I starte
to set up in preparation for the midwife to arrive, bu
it soon became apparent that this baby was comin
now and I was going to have to catch it.

Vickie was on the bed, and all of a sudden sh
moved down onto the floor. She was squatting an

ushing, and soon his head was born. A couple more ushes. For some reason his body would not come ut. Time is critical when the head is born because he neck is being compressed and the baby needs o come out. I knew Vickie needed to change her osition so that I could assist the baby out.

I told Brett to pick her up and turn her around. He looked at me and said, "What?" I repeated to turn er around, and together we moved her. Now I could et my hands positioned where I could ease the baby ut. When he emerged he was not breathing. Inwardly was a little panicked, but on the outside I was cool as cucumber. In my mind I began to pray and grabbed he oxygen. When Brett saw that the baby was not reathing he looked afraid, but almost immediately e seemed at peace. I rubbed the baby's chest and ut the oxygen under his nose. Thank goodness I had rought it! Very quickly he took a breath and started o cry. He was in good condition and started to nurse. I remember correctly, Elisha weighed 10 pounds and vas 23 inches long.

Elisha was a big baby, and sometimes big babies et their shoulders stuck. Changing position can widen he pelvis and allow moving the shoulders enough that he child can be born. I think that is what happened n this case. Soon after the birth the midwife showed p, and she checked out mom and baby. Both were loing well.

Chapter 15
Making Memories

There are many births that I remember wel
Sometimes I remember because it was a challenge
such as with Elisha, and sometimes I remembe
because of humor or an unexpected occurrence.

I worked with a woman named Gina who wa
hearing impaired but read lips. She came to m
childbirth classes, and she and her husband aske
me to be at their hospital birth. Her baby wa
breech, meaning she was coming butt first. We ha
not been able to change her position, so a skille
doctor at the hospital was necessary.

Gina labored pretty peacefully and quietl
When transition hits (those last few centimeters c
dilation) it's not unusual to see a shift in mood of th
mom. She was still quiet, but when I gave her ic
chips she handed them back to me and told me t
"save them for later." Aha! She was in transition!
was incredible to see the doctor deliver the baby bu
first. Most breech babies are born with a c-sectior
It is usually safer for both mom and baby, howeve
this doctor had lots of experience, and this baby gi
was born with no complications. The picture that
clearest in my mind is the baby laying in the warmin
bed with her legs pointed up along her body. Sh
had been in that position so long in the womb that
would take a while for her legs to come down. Sh
was beautiful, and this was such a joyful birth.

I've been asked to do many things as a midwife, but I never expected to be asked if I could check out a pregnant goat. I explained to the Amish farmer that it wasn't quite the same anatomy as a human and I wouldn't be of much help. Another couple asked me to stop at the store and pick up a gallon of milk on my way to their house. After doing a prenatal visit at an Amish home, Lois asked me if I would help her pick beans in the garden. She was barefoot so I kicked off my shoes and joined her in walking through the cool dirt, picking produce. Needless to say, I went home with an abundance of beans and corn that day. As I mentioned previously, if you are the midwife to the community you are treated like a member. Sometimes that even means doing chores.

I had the pleasure of working with a young Amish couple with three children. Everytime I went to their house I had a new and sometimes comic experience. Mary was very friendly and lighthearted. She had to be to put up with her husband. He was a bit of a scalawag—Jonah said he was always being reprimanded by the church leaders for some misdeed. He was a little bit rebellious and liked to put extra reflectors on his buggy. The elders told him he was being too flashy and trying to bring attention to himself. He was advised to repent and take the larger reflectors off the buggy. Then there was the time he was discovered with a transistor radio in his barn. He enjoyed country music but, of course, this was not allowed. A neighbor who visited him heard the music and reported him to the elders. Another reprimand. Jonah also liked to hint at an off-color joke or an inappropriate remark. One day after a prenatal visit he hitched a ride with me to his mailbox about a half mile away. In the car he asked how soon he could resume relations with his wife after the baby was born. I gave him a professional answer in a quiet voice and, much to my surprise, he reached over and put his hand on my thigh. I slapped his hand away and said, "You don't touch the midwife!" He laughed and pretended it was all a joke. In spite of this particular transgression, I really enjoyed their company and always left them feeling upbeat.

Many Amish families live in areas that are somewhat difficult to get to in the winter. Narrow gravel roads don't always get plowed after a snowstorm, and some homes are deep in a valley. One winter I had a client in such a location. At a prenatal visit we discussed what to do if the weather was bad when it was time for the baby. It was agreed I would park my car at the top of the ridge where they would see my headlights. Sure enough, the night she went into labor there was quite a mountain of snow. The father had ridden his horse to the neighbors to call me, and when I arrived I had to load all of my equipment onto the horse. He took my stuff to the house, and then came back for me. I limbed on the hood of my car to be tall enough to get on the horse. Down into the valley we rode with snow flurries all around us. It was like something out of a storybook. This was one of those magical moments that I was so privileged to be a part of.

Carpentry and furniture making are skills possessed by many Amish men. Their homes have beautiful furnishings that have been made by themselves or another member of the community. I once had an Amish-made rocking chair that was a treasured possession. Made from hickory, it was strong and curved to fit my back. Many hours were spent rocking and relaxing. One day I went for a prenatal at the home of a young woman named Ruth and noticed a small chest of drawers. I asked her who made it and found out it was her uncle who lived not too far away. She suggested I stop by his place and speak with him about making one for me. Amish are very private people and not necessarily open to strangers stopping by. When I pulled into her uncle's driveway, he and a small boy were sitting on the front step. They both wore black pants, blue shirts with suspenders, and black hats. The man kept his head down and did not look at me. I told him I was at Ruth's house and she told me to stop and ask him about furniture. He didn't say anything for a moment and then asked, "What was ya doin' at Ruth's?" I replied I was Ruth's midwife, and he raised his head, looked me in the eye and said, "Oh! So

you're the midwife!" He reached out to shake m
hand and led me back to his workshop. I was so
impressed with the furniture he was working on.
told him what I wanted, and we agreed on a price
A few weeks later I received word the chest wa
finished, and when I went to pick it up he would no
take any money for it. He said it was a thank you gif
for all I was doing for their young mothers. Anothe
example of why I love the spirit and generosity o
this gentle and kind culture.

My midwifery philosophy is to let the body de
what it knows how to do. If we let nature take it
course, most of the time all will be well. Allowing
mom freedom to move and position herself as she
feels comfortable means that she is utilizing gravit
to help open her pelvis and make more room fo
the baby to pass through. Midwives have concocted
all kinds of furniture and apparatus to assist i
positioning. One midwife I know took the seat off a
kitchen chair, wrapped the frame with foam, and wa
able to catch the baby from underneath while Mom
was seated. Pretty cool, but cumbersome.

I was describing this chair to a Mennonite fathe
and said I wished for something like that but shorte
I wanted a stool that would put the mother in more
of a squatting position without all the strain on he
legs. He told me he thought he could build a stoo
for me, and I took him up on his offer. At my nex
prenatal visit he was anxious to show me what he

had made. When he presented me with the stool, I cried. It was beautiful and very functional. He made it low to the ground and cut out a curve in the seat so a baby could be born while mom was on the stool. Most women have labored on it for a while, but not given birth on it. It's a wonderful tool for labor. I still have it, and now it holds my sock monkey collection! This is the stool in the photograph on the cover of this book.

Chapter 16
Theresa's Story

Theresa and her husband participated in th first set of classes I taught in my home office. Ove the course of 12 weeks we became friends, and the asked me to be their midwife and help them hav the home birth they desired. They both had realisti expectations, and Theresa was a healthy woman wit very low risk factors. Preparations had been made and I waited for the call.

Eva Arrives

"Renee delivered our beautiful baby girl at ou home in the country. My husband and I attende prenatal classes in preparation for the home birt taught by Renee. We are well-educated people an are very conscious of making informed decision throughout our life and did not want childbirth to b any different. Thanks to Renee it wasn't.

"Renee's classes were well organized and fille with lots of practical information she obviously use and understood, not just memorized from a book Renee taught the information and gave possibilitie for dealing with various situations, but left th decisions up to the parents. The atmosphere of th class was friendly, sharing, and constructive. Rene stressed developing a working relationship with you partner that allowed us to practice communicatin and being sensitive to each other's needs BEFOR the crisis of delivery. There was a beautiful balance between factual, high-tech information and the emotional ups and downs of pregnancy, delivery, and parenting. By the end of the class we felt ready for all the possibilities because we had thought out and talked about how we would handle each one. We were secure in the knowledge that we could work through whatever happened together.

"Eva's birth started with labor pains that were very close together and hard. I was fully dilated after only two hours, and the contractions were so strong right from the beginning that I couldn't stand up during them even with my husband's support. I remember feeling like I was drowning in the sensations and worried whether I could last through it. One of the first things Renee said when she got there (during a contraction of course) was, "You're doing great. It's almost over; hang in there." The idea that the contractions were, after all, only a minute or two long and then you got a rest was a life saver. Renee supported my husband and I working together rather than stepping in and taking over. She let us have the experience we had worked together to get but was always there when either of us needed a suggestion or support to make the experience a very high quality. I never worried about the baby because I trusted Renee's ability to handle complications and she kept me informed of the baby's heartbeat throughout delivery. I felt this freed me to concentrate more on feeling the rhythms of the delivery.

"My husband and I both felt that Eva's birth was a great experience, but without Renee we would have been frightened and might have panicked because it was so strong. Renee, as a midwife, was the perfect balance between getting us through the experience so it was ours by mothering us when we needed it and being very professional when we needed that."

Chapter 17
Grace and David

Grace was a lovely young Amish woman who was expecting her first child. Her husband David was a farmer and occasionally hired himself out for construction projects. Grace kept a large garden and sold some of her produce at a roadside stand. They were excited about the upcoming birth, but understandably nervous as this was their first. David found me by asking another Amish man who had several children and had used my services previously. I received a letter in the mail asking me to stop by the next time I was in the area.

I sent a letter setting a date, and when I arrived they invited me into their small but cozy home. I always tried to make my visits during the day so we could have adequate lighting. At night the homes are lit with kerosene lanterns and give off a warm glow. Daylight better allowed me to write my notes as I asked about her medical history and other pertinent information.

Grace was healthy and strong, and I expected no complications when the time came for her to give birth. When her labor pains began David called me from a neighbor's house, and I packed my birth kit and hit the road. Grace was in active labor when I got there and was walking back and forth in her large garden.

Amish women like to remain as active as possibl
during labor, as they know labor will progress quicke
than if they stay in the bed. When the labor pain
became more difficult to deal with, Grace wante
to sit with her feet in a pan of water. Her mothe
had told her this would be helpful. I didn't believ
it myself, but there was no harm in having a goo
foot soak. Throughout the contractions Grace wa
very quiet and never made any complaint. I had t
watch her for signs that labor was changing, sinc
she was not verbalizing what she was feeling. A
one point she looked at me with glazed eyes, an
I knew I needed to check her for dilation. She wa
ready to birth this baby.

By now it was dark outside, and David had l
a lamp in the living room and one in the bedroom
Grace got onto the bed, and David knelt beside he
It was several pushes before the baby's head wa
ready to be born. Still, Grace had been quiet. Wit
the next push the head was out, and the followin
push brought the rest of the body. Sarah had bee
born. While I was attending to the baby, David go
into the bed with Grace, and I handed them thei
new family member. Amish women are covered eve
during birth, so there was no full skin-to-skin contact
but Grace opened her dress, and Sarah began t
nurse. I had never seen an Amish father get int
the bed before, and I was deeply touched by thi
sight before me. The birth had been so gentle and

uiet, and in the soft glow of the lamp, there was n obvious abundance of love. The peacefulness of his labor and birth, along with the dedication of the father, has never left me and always brings tears to my eyes as I recall it.

Chapter 18
Sharing With Nurses

One of the things I really loved was when hospital would ask me to come and speak abou doulas or midwifery or working with other culture The Amish are a totally different culture than mos of us experience, and their birthing practices ca teach us about birthing without pain medication. simply isn't available to them, and they are mentall prepared to work with their bodies and not figh against the pain that comes.

There was a women's hospital that used t invite me about once a year to come and speak to large group of nurses about home birthing with th Amish. The nurses were accustomed to attendin labors in which pain medication and epidural were common. If a laboring mom expressed he desire for medication-free labor, the nurses wer sometimes skeptical and didn't necessarily kno how to best help mom achieve that. The hospit felt that hearing about Amish labors and how the prepared and managed without medication woul give the nurse insight on how they could best hel their patients achieve their goal. The nurses wer receptive and seemed to really enjoy hearing abou my experiences and learning new coping technique I always looked forward to these presentations an getting feedback when they were able to work wit a laboring mom with a new point of view.

Chapter 19
Lady in Labor

Lady was expecting her first child and had chosen to have her baby in a hospital with an obstetrician. She asked me to be with her and her husband as a friend and to help ease the jitters. I was honored to be asked. First time parents are often anxious, and I wanted to do what I could to help even though I was not there in my midwife capacity. Unexpectedly, it turned out to be a test for me.

Lady's Story

"It was most certainly one of the longest days I can remember. In the hospital, three weeks before my due date, we'd gone from what felt like a surreal sense of urgency due to pre-eclampsia, to the 15th hour of waiting. Even after being induced, my son wasn't budging. We went from an eternity of nothing happening, to all of a sudden everything was happening at once. I was now wearing an oxygen mask, and the doctors were having trouble getting a heartbeat from my baby. His heartbeat was going from faint, to nonexistent, to faint again. Renee was a midwife but was there as my friend and to support my husband through the process. But in all honesty, I know she was there to help me deliver a healthy baby. After what seemed like a lifetime of pushing with nothing happening, I remember having heightened clarity as I watched my doctor grow alarmed. The doctor turned to the OB nurse and told her to prepare a room for emergency C-section. I don't think I'd gotten truly afraid that it could all go wrong until then. I started praying. I don't know if I was praying aloud, but all I could concentrate on was asking God to save my baby, to make sure he would arrive healthy, and even prayers that if God was only going to save one of us that He would save this new, precious baby boy of mine.

"All the hustle and bustle in my room was evidence that the doctor and nurses thought the emergency cesarean section was the only way to go. What happened next was quite extraordinary. My very "by the modern medical book" doctor asked Renee, who she'd learned a bit about throughout the morning, "What would you do?" All I can remember from that point was Renee and my husband holding my legs and putting me into some kind of pretzel position. The doctor told me to push, push, stop, push again. There was no need for the C-section.

"My baby son was born absolutely perfect. Over eight pounds and nearly 21 inches. I have no doubt in my mind that Renee, my friend and midwife, being in my room was not a coincidence. More like an answer to a prayer I didn't know I'd need answered. Yes and Amen."

My Recollection

Throughout the morning Lady's doctor was in and out of the room, and we got to know each other slightly. Lady told her I was a midwife, and I wasn't sure I wanted the doctor to know that. I never know what kind of reception I will receive from a medical doctor, and so I tend not to announce it. Lady's doctor was welcoming and seemed curious. We didn't have a chance to discuss it, and I assumed the issue had passed.

Lady was beginning to push, and as she did, the baby's heart rate began to respond to the contractions in a manner that told us the baby was being overly stressed. After a few more pushes and more evidence that the baby's heartbeat was slowing, the doctor said a cesarean section surgery was necessary to get the baby out quickly. As the nurse was scurrying to make arrangements for the operating room, the doctor turned to me and asked, "What would you do?"

I was taken aback and inwardly began to pray, "Oh Lord, if I am ever to have a correct answer, let it be now!" I responded that I would change her position in order to open Lady's pelvis wider and give more room for the baby to come out. The doctor had a surprised look on her face and said, "Really?" I explained that since Lady was on her back her pelvis was being compressed which was making it more difficult for the baby to move through the birth canal. I instructed Lady, her husband, and the docto how we were going to position her, and so we did We moved her into an upright squat which allowed gravity to help the baby descend and be born.

It was such a relief that a cesarean section wa not needed. The doctor seemed amazed that my suggestion actually worked, and when a colleague of hers stuck her head in the door to see how thing were going, the doctor replied as she pointed to me "She taught me something new!" I felt so gratified that not only was Lady spared a surgery, but that the doctor learned a new technique that she would probably use at another birth.

Chapter 20
Ciera and Gage

I've attended so many births over the years and have lost count of just how many. Each one was special and touched me in some way. Some were scary, some were incredibly peaceful, and some were very personal. I am blessed to have two beautiful grandchildren, and at times it was a balancing act to be both midwife and grandma. I'd like to share both of those very special birth stories. My daughter Abby shared her recollections and mine will follow.

Abby's Story: Ciera's Birth

"For as long as I can remember, I wanted to be a mom. I wanted four kids, two boys and two girls. I was eighteen when I became pregnant with my daughter. I truly had no idea I was pregnant. I was taking the test to get my coworker to stop telling me I was pregnant. Wow! What a shock it was when that blue plus sign showed up! I was absolutely stunned, yet immediately happy. I couldn't wait to get to my fiance, Cliff, to tell him the news.

"My pregnancy was one hurdle after the other the entire time, but my (our) excitement stayed full throttle right up to the morning my water broke at three and a half weeks early. I was scared because it was too soon for her to arrive, and my mom was still in Wisconsin and we were living in Oklahoma. I woke up thinking I had peed the bed, but as I waddled to

79

the bathroom I felt a gush and realized right awa
that my water had broken and that's what had woke
me up. Cliff called my mom and brought me th
phone as I sat on the toilet not knowing what to do
I remember mom being so calm and reassuring m
that my baby was going to be okay, that she wasn
coming too early. Mom asked me several question:
calmed me down and told us to go to the hospit
and that she would be on her way.

"Once I was admitted and checked, then m
excitement was back. We're doing this— we'r
having our baby today! The doctor gave me a firr
time limit of twelve hours after my water brok
for labor to start on its own. While we paced th
maternity ward floor, rocked in a rocking chair, an
rolled on the giant yoga ball, mom was on her way t
Oklahoma. I remember being happy but frustrate
as the hours ticked by and still no sign of labor. A
one point while I was in my bed taking a break fror
all of the walking, Cliff and I played cards. We fe
prepared; we had attended birthing classes, and
knew a lot because my mom was a midwife. I don
recall when mom got there, but we were all so happ
that she made it in time.

"Once the twelve hours were up and labor hadn
started no matter how much walking and rocking
was doing, I was given Pitocin to start my labor.
wasn't allowed to get out of bed, and I was alread
worn out from the walking, my super early morninɡ

and nothing to eat since the previous night. I asked for crackers and was told absolutely not. Coming into this I had decided that I really wanted to have the birth be as natural as I could manage. I didn't want an epidural, I didn't want pain meds, I didn't want them to just do whatever and not talk with me or Cliff about it first. We had a vision of what we hoped birth would be. Our vision was turning into a nightmare.

"The Pitocin had my contractions coming rapidly and with very little break in between. There came a point when I said I wanted pain medicine. I don't remember when I got it, if I only asked once or gave it another try first, but I did get it. Once that sweet relief hit me I was ready. I remember saying I can do this. That was very short lived. I don't know how long it took for the pain to be overwhelming again, but I demanded another dose right exactly when the clock hands hit the "you can't have anymore until _____ time has passed." At one point I hallucinated an eight foot tall Smurf standing at the foot of my bed. I couldn't believe no one else saw him!

"My contractions were so close together and lasted so long. I just wanted to be done with this. I don't know how long I pushed. During one push, I screamed. A nurse told me to calm down and quiet down. I screamed because there was a very distinct, completely different pain. Not only was it unbearable, but I thought for sure something was

81

wrong. I told them what I had felt and where I felt it. Something is wrong! I was chastised, and my worries were completely ignored.

"When my baby was finally born, she wasn't breathing. I didn't get to hold her longer than it took to cut the cord. She was taken to the NICU as soon as they had her breathing. But my torment wasn't over. The doctor, who wasn't my doctor, just the on-call doctor, didn't wait for the afterbirth to come on its own. The doctor wrapped the cord around his hand, braced his foot, and pulled it out of me. On top of the very unnecessary pain this caused, this ripping of the afterbirth caused me to hemorrhage. I ended up staying two extra nights in the hospital because of this.

It was almost three hours after birth that my daughter was brought back to me. I remember sitting in the chair holding her and thinking, what now? Where was the magical bonding that I was promised? She and I were alone in the room and I felt like I was broken.

"I knew that labor and delivery were going to be a pain like I had never experienced. I had no misconceptions about the whole process. What I experienced was beyond anything that I had worked so hard to prepare for. I swore I would never have another baby. I wouldn't go through any of that again. People laughed and told me that's what every first time mom says and that I would forget the pain and change my mind. No. This was not the regular declaration of first time moms; I was serious, and I did not forget or change my mind.

"I was angry at how the whole experience had gone and how much pain I was in afterwards head to toe. I could barely function and had not bonded with my baby. Thankfully, my mom was able to stay with me for a few weeks. My daughter barely nursed, it was as if she didn't want or like my milk. After a couple of weeks we were told by the baby doctor that if we didn't switch to formula they were going to admit her to the hospital for jaundice. I was devastated. I had never even considered formula. I knew absolutely that I would breastfeed my baby. This was another crushing blow.

"I developed postpartum depression quite severely. Mom had to return to Wisconsin, my husband (we had married over Christmas break) had to get back to full time college and work, and in my mind, my baby didn't want me. She wouldn't nurse, she wouldn't sleep, she had health problems, and we hadn't bonded. On most days I would set up a supply of bottles of water, a can of formula, a stack of diapers and wipes on my headboard and I'd stay in bed with her the entire day until just before Cliff came home. I don't remember how long this lasted or when I finally felt a bond with her, but even when I no longer felt tormented daily and I was head over heels for my precious girl, I still was certain that I would not have another baby, ever."

My Recollection

When Abby announced she was pregnant, my first reaction was disbelief, but I quickly came to be very excited. My first grandchild! I soon realized that since we lived in different states, I would not get to be a part of her pregnancy except for telephone calls. Because of the distance I could not be her midwife—I was the grandma.

Abby had learned a lot about pregnancy through the years because I was always open with her about my work as a midwife. She helped me prepare for childbirth classes, and I think she even attended some when I was just beginning to teach. felt she had a great attitude about labor and delivery and would prepare herself by reading and speaking with her doctor. She always filled me in after each prenatal visit, and we discussed any questions she had or concerns as they came up. I so wanted to be there, but I had to settle for going to Oklahoma when her due date arrived. She never made it to that day.

I received an early morning call from Cliff telling me that Abby's water had broken, and I had to quickly wake up to talk to her, reassure her, and help her to calm herself. It was three and a half weeks before her due date, and she was scared. I told her I would be on my way as soon as I could make arrangements. I had to make some calls and get someone to drive

me all the way to Chicago to catch a plane. By the
me I arrived in Tulsa it was late afternoon, and Abby
was in active labor when I got to the hospital.

She had been given Pitocin to stimulate her
labor, and those kinds of managed labors can be
very challenging. Contractions tend to be harder
and more difficult to cope with. The midwife part of
me knew things could have gone another way, but
due to distance and time, Abby was in the hands of
an obstetrician. I could not interfere, but I did try
to comfort and reassure Abby. I spoke with her and
touched her and tried to soothe her pain.

She was really suffering and at one point looked
down at her belly and growled, "Get this child out of
me!" It was like a scene from The Exorcist. I was so
upset that she was having a traumatic experience,
and it was triggering my own birth experience when
I had her. I knew we had to get her through this and
deal with the aftermath. Baby Ciera was born with
a breathing issue that was safely monitored, and
within days mom and baby went home.

I was able to stay a few weeks and tried to
help Abby get established into a routine with the
baby. Unfortunately, Ciera did not want to nurse.
As a lactation consultant we used my bag of tricks
and were not successful. As I recall, we asked a
consultant from the hospital to pay a visit, and she
also was not able to get Ciera to nurse. It was as
if Ciera was allergic to the breast milk. She would

projectile vomit and seemed to be in pain. She developed jaundice, and the doctor wanted Abby to switch to formula and see if that changed things. It did.

Ciera took formula and stopped vomiting and crying so much. Abby was disappointed as she had always planned on nursing, but in the end a healthy baby was the most important thing—and for some reason, that seemed to be with formula. This difficulty with nursing contributed to Abby depression, and she had to come to terms with her birth experience. It was hard to do, and she was certain she would never have another child. I totally understood, as it mimicked my own birth experience and trauma and was why I only had one child. I knew if she ever changed her mind that we would have to work closely to have a more satisfying experience.

Abby's Story: Gage's Birth

"When our baby girl was about seven month old, we had just moved back to Wisconsin. Now that we had family around, we were going to have a night out with friends. My period was a week late so I wanted to take a pregnancy test just to be sure I wasn't pregnant before we went out for drinks that night. I didn't feel pregnant, and I wasn't having any symptoms other than my period hadn't started. But a late period was enough for me to want to double check before drinking.

"I called the local pregnancy crisis center in our little hometown and got an appointment for that afternoon. My husband dropped me off and was going to wait in the car since we figured it would just be a quick confirmation that we were in the clear. I took the test and could not believe it when there was more than a blue negative sign showing up! It didn't develop into a plus sign, but it was more than just a negative. What!? I tried to convince the counselor that because it wasn't a clear plus, it had to be negative. It just had to be! I remember feeling shock and denial. It took quite a while for me to believe the test was positive, that I was pregnant again. My reaction to finding out I was pregnant was the opposite reaction I had when learning about my first pregnancy. I wasn't excited, I was devastated. My first pregnancy and birth was so traumatic, I swore I'd never do it again.

"When I finally walked outside I didn't see Cliff anywhere. He ran a quick errand since I was taking longer than expected. I was standing at the corner and must have looked unusual because pretty soon I heard someone call my name and come running across the street. It was an old friend of mine, and when he got to me he asked what was wrong. My tears started all over again, and I said, 'I'm pregnant.'

"My feelings about another pregnancy were so incredibly different from how I felt the first time.

Instead of immediate elation, I had a moment of wishing I felt differently about abortion. I didn't seriously consider it, not even for a second, and still, 25 years later, I feel badly that the subject even crossed my mind. It took a few hours for the shock and denial to work its way through my mind, but when it did I accepted that our family was growing, ready or not, and started falling in love with this new baby. By the end of the night we were celebrating our new addition.

"Everything about this pregnancy was different from my first experience. I didn't have any complications and felt as good as a pregnant mom with a one year old could hope to feel. Every checkup showed myself and the baby doing well. Throughout this pregnancy my mom did her best to assure me that this labor and delivery would be a much different experience than the first one. Mom and I only lived a few hours apart instead of several states, so even if my labor started early, she'd be able to be there—and this time she'd be able to help me more as a midwife instead of a first-time grandma. My husband and I were comforted knowing that mom would be there to make sure I didn't have another nightmare
experience.

"My last prenatal check happened when I was three days past my due date. Baby and I were healthy, and I was dilated to three centimeters.

I called my mom after the appointment to give her the latest update. We had already talked about options for starting labor if needed, and as far as I was concerned, it was now needed. She went over the information with me again on what to do, and then she was on her way to us. I drank castor oil and waited. After the allotted time I drank the second dose. Still to this day, if I see, smell, or think too long about castor oil, I start to heave. It was so worth it though.

"Mom arrived and our evening was going on like normal, except for a few more trips to the bathroom for me. I started having contractions that night, but they were sporadic. It was well after midnight when we all decided to try and sleep since the contractions were not coming any faster or lasting longer. Our daughter had already been asleep for several hours by then. My husband went to bed, mom settled on the couch, and I needed the bathroom one more time before heading to my bed. I felt like I was going to have another bowel movement, but nothing was happening. I felt different, no other way to explain it, just different.

"Mom knocked on the door and asked to come in. I guess she saw or heard something that made her say this was it! I was in transition, and we needed to go now. Right now! I remember her telling Cliff to grab a flashlight. I don't remember who grabbed our daughter, or even getting to the car, but I do remember mom telling Cliff to go faster and if no cars were coming to go ahead and run the stoplights. My contractions were coming fast and hard. Each time I felt one coming I grabbed the handle above the door with one hand and pushed myself off the seat with the other hand. I wanted to push so bad it felt like the baby was right there! We pulled up at the emergency room door, and I waddled in and told the nurses that I was having my baby RIGHT NOW! I was put in a wheelchair and whisked away.

"As the nurses were pulling the delivery bed apart and getting the room ready, I told them I didn't want to wait any longer—I needed to push. During this time my mom, my husband, and my 16 month old daughter made it to my room. It was almost 3:00 a.m. I was dilated to ten, and the nurses still didn't want me to push. The doctor wasn't there and they hadn't gotten the monitor on my belly. My contractions were close, and I wanted to get on with it. Mom was talking me through the contractions and reassuring me.

"Then it was time. The doc was in the room and I pushed with the next contraction. I sat myself upright, turned to face my husband, locked eyes with him, and actually smiled at him. I gave a big push, and my water broke. I was making little yelping sounds and then a little scream. Mom told me the head was right there. My little girl started to cry; I'm sure my pain scared her. I looked over at her nd told her it was okay, that I was okay, and she topped crying. The contraction was still going, and ny mom said 'lots of hair' which made me smile.

"Mom was running a big old-fashioned amcorder, coaching me, and telling me what she vas seeing. I gave a second push, and the baby's ead was out. I was smiling and saying, "Oh baby!" he nurse said, "It's a boy." My husband about did backflip at the news! All three of us were so happy. Gage started crying right away, and I said, "Listen o him!" Mom was thanking God and telling my laughter that she had a baby brother. The cord was ut and then my baby boy was handed to me, crying is beautiful little heart out. We were all so happy nd laughing—I even stuck my tongue out at the amera.

"About an hour and twenty minutes after the ontractions started, and three pushes, I was holding ny son. Mom carried my daughter to Cliff so she ould be right there and see her new brother. I told ne doctor I wanted the placenta to come on its wn, and we can see in the video that's exactly what appened.

"Everything about this birth was vastly different om the first one. This time there was no fear, no eeling of helplessness, no trauma. I can't imagine a nore joyous delivery room. This was more like the xperience we had wished for when we had Ciera. I emember saying that this was as easy as childbirth

can be, and I can understand why women are alrigh
with doing it a few times."

My Recollection

When Abby told me she was pregnant again
I knew I would have to work very closely with he
to overcome the trauma she experienced whe
Ciera was born. There is such a strong mind-bod
connection that I knew if her thoughts were c
fear and apprehension, her body would respon
accordingly. I wanted her to be happy and joyfu
about this upcoming labor and delivery. We sti
lived in different states, even though I was closer th
time around. Because of the distance, she was goin
to have a local doctor and make a hospital plan fc
delivery. All of her prenatal visits were going wel
and she was encouraged.

We spoke of how we could create a differer
labor and birth experience. I gave her relaxatio
techniques to practice, and we made a plan to tal
often on the phone. She kept me updated, an
with each call, I was able to reassure and encourag
her. Being physically active in labor can really b
helpful, so walking, rocking, using a birth ball, an
changing positions often were put on her list c
possible activities. Clearly, I was to take on the rol
of midwife much more than I had been able to wit
Ciera's birth.

She went past her due date with nothing happening, but when she went for a prenatal visit she was told she was three centimeters dilated and her cervix was soft. Since she was already overdue, we decided that I would intervene in a way that would help her labor start. We set up a schedule for her to take castor oil, and I would make my way to her. Castor oil has been used by midwives for decades, and if there is dilation and the cervix is ripe and soft, castor oil can start labor. Sometimes it doesn't work, and in that case, mom spends a lot of time in the bathroom cleaning out her system. In Abby's case, it was going to be worth a try.

I arrived at her house, and not much was happening. She had made several trips to the bathroom, but contractions were mild and she wasn't having much discomfort, except for the diarrhea. We all decided to try and sleep, so she headed for the bathroom one last time before bed. I heard Abby call for me, and she said she felt different. I listened to the sounds she was making and realized she was in transition and that we had to head to the hospital.

Abby had not planned to have the baby at home. We woke Ciera and had to bring her with us since everything was now happening so quickly and there was no one she could stay with. As we headed out the door I told Cliff to grab a flashlight. In my mind I thought there was a chance this baby would be born before we made it to the hospital. Because it was late at night there was no traffic, and I told Cliff to safely run the stoplights and get us to the hospital asap. I did not want to catch the baby on the side of the road!

Within minutes of arriving at the hospital Abby was in a room wanting to push. Amazingly enough, she was smiling between contractions and assuring Ciera that she was alright and that the baby would be here soon. Abby even laughed between contractions. This was in stark contrast to her 'exorcist moments' when she birthed Ciera. Three pushes later and Gage was born! So much joy, laughter and excitement! Everything about this labor and delivery was what Abby had hoped for. The trauma of Ciera's birth was overshadowed by this miraculous and peaceful experience.

Abby bonded with Gage immediately, and believe it's because there was no trauma, including the trauma of being separated from her baby as she had been with Ciera. Gage nursed right from the beginning, and Abby was able to breastfeed for many months without any difficulty. As I mentioned before, there is a strong mind-body connection, and the difficulty of Ciera's birth and Abby's reaction to it may have been a contributing factor as to why Ciera was not able to breastfeed.

It was hard to be both grandma and midwife at each of Abby's births. I did what I could under each circumstance, and while I wish I could have done more, two beautiful children were born, and I am so proud to be called 'Grandma.'

Chapter 21
Russian Rendezvous

In light of my experiences with both Amis and "English" families, I was thrilled when anothe cultural initiative came my way. I was accepted int a program which would give me educational an clinical experiences as a midwife in St. Petersburg Russia. My excitement at being a participant in thi cultural endeavor had me counting down the day until I made the journey of 5000 miles. Russia wa such a foreign land to me and I knew very little factua information. I was so excited but also afraid. Woul the hardships and difficulties I had read about be tru for me? How would I communicate? What would eat? Would I be cold? Was danger going to be i my path? There was so much unknown to me but wanted the challenge and the adventure. I was read to take a calculated risk and by doing so, my life woul completely change. I first went to Russia in 1992 an chaos was the order of the day. It was the time c perestroika and glasnost which means restructurin and openness. Russia had just begun to welcome th rest of the world and times were challenging. Toda there is more stability.

I am excited to say that I am currently working o a book to share the wonderful stories and grea adventures of my times in Russia! I want to shar with my readers a little bit about the night before m Russian journey began and give just a taste of wha will be coming in my next book.

Day One of My Diary

"Today the journey begins and for just a moment towards the end of the evening, I wonder what I have gotten myself into. Is it possible that tomorrow I will travel to Russia? Can it be real that I am going to work in a country that I have always feared? In school I was taught that Russia was our enemy and I had read stories about people disappearing, never to be heard from again. I didn't know how much of that was true but I was willing to take some chances. Now, here I am, about to spend the next few months in St. Petersburg working as a midwife. I'm so excited but have to admit, I feel some fear and anxiety.

Today I arrived in Chicago to spend the night at the home of the trip organizer. Tomorrow we leave and it was arranged for us to have a brief orientation tonight. When I was dropped off at the home I was pleasantly surprised to find two of the other midwives were already here. There were five of us that would be traveling from different parts of the United States for this Russian maternity opportunity. These ladies were from California, New Mexico, Wisconsin and Texas. They all were very experienced and I hoped to expand my knowledge and skills by working with and learning from them. Everyone had different plans for how long they would be staying in Russia, from a minimum of six weeks to a maximum of twelve.

This afternoon a Russian woman named Mari
came over to tell us a bit about Russian life. W
were all ears. Maria and her family came to th
United States about 18 months ago seeking politica
asylum. They are Jewish and it was dangerous fo
them to remain in Russia. The United States was on
of many countries offering shelter to Russian Jew:
Maria was a physical therapist by profession althoug
she could not work as one here in the U.S. withou
further training and credentialing. I saw before me
very pretty woman with short dark hair but I also sa
pain in her eyes. Here in the U.S. she prefers to b
called Mary and she is 26 years old. She tells us he
life has been very difficult and as she begins to te
us her stories, there is much pain in her words.

Life for the Russian woman is so hard. Almos
all of them have jobs outside their home but the
are also responsible for cooking, cleaning, shoppin
and caring for children. They wait in long lines afte
work to buy the food that they need. It is tiresom
and takes a lot of time. Mostly, the men do not hel
with domestic duties.

The majority of the money a family earns goe
to pay for food and it is barely enough. Mary recentl
heard from a friend in Moscow who told her that the
were without heat and she was fearful it could be fc
the entire winter.

Mary spoke of the birth of one of her children. She told how after her child was born, she was taken to a room to be stitched. She believes this procedure took about one and a half hours and that it was done with no anesthesia, which to her was like being tortured. Mary is convinced it was done this way so she would remember her hospital stay and never come back. The doctor who performed this procedure died of cancer five years later and Mary thinks maybe this was punishment for the doctor who treated her so harshly.

The maternity hospitals, called roddoms, are free of charge. Only the elite can afford to go to a private hospital. This costs about 16,000 rubles which is about $40 American. Mary states the difference in care is totally opposite and I will find out for myself as I will be working in both types.

Mary gave us lots of information about obstetrical care and I wonder how much of what she says is her own opinion as opposed to fact. I guess I will find that out for myself also.

She tells us most pregnant women suffer from toxemia and what she calls a "tense uterus." I can't wait to find out what that actually means. We were shocked to hear that most women have had anywhere from three to nine abortions without anesthesia. There is virtually no birth control and a woman at age 26 is considered old to be having her first baby because it probably means she has had several abortions.

Maternity leave is paid for two months before and after the birth. They are paid less than full pay for being on maternity leave for the next year and a half. The government supports family life by making this payment available.

Women breastfeed their babies but some lose their milk. This is due to stress and environmental factors. In the roddoms milk is taken from each woman and is shared.

Mary tells us she will never go back to Russia. She has a hard time understanding why anyone would want to go there. At least I know I can return home.

According to Mary, nationalism is on the rise. This means anti-Semitism and racism. This accounts for why so many Jewish families apply for asylum to other countries. People have lost their jobs and their housing for the simple fact of their religion. She believes the current political policy of openness is just empty words. Yes, there are a few more freedoms but most things are the same. One of the biggest problems is that people cannot make decisions for themselves, it has always been done for them.

I can't get to sleep because my mind keeps replaying everything that Mary has told us. I am fearful, anxious but yet, I am excited."

While I have just told of difficulties and hardships, my experience was also of those things but more of wonder, friendships, romance, teaching, catching babies, travel and the so-called Russian mafia. I can't wait to share those stories with you in my next book.

Epilogue

I have been blessed and honored to have been invited into the Amish and Mennonite communities to help their young families. I learned so much from them, and they helped to change the way I saw labor and birth. They are a culture within our own "English" culture, and I loved my experiences with them. It was fascinating to learn how another culture views pregnancy and birth, especially where it differed so much from what I was accustomed to.